D0098105

Schenck v. United States

Restrictions on Free Speech

Karen Alonso

Landmark Supreme Court Cases

Enslow Publishers, Inc.

40 Industrial Road	PO Box 38
Box 398	Aldershot
Berkeley Heights, NJ 07922	Hants GU12 6BP
USA	UK

http://www.enslow.com

Library of Congress Cataloging-in-Publication Data

Alonso, Karen.
    Schenck v. United States: restrictions on free speech / Karen Alonso.
      p. cm. — (Landmark Supreme Court cases)
    Includes bibliographical references and index.
    Summary: Describes the landmark case that limited free speech in cases of "clear and
present danger" to national security, as well as later cases that continued working out the
limits of freedom of speech.
    ISBN 0-7660-1089-9
    1. Freedom of speech—United States—Juvenile literature. 2. Sedition—United
States—Juvenile literature. 3. Schenck, Charles—Trials, litigation, etc.—Juvenile
literature. 4. Trials (Sedition)—Pennsylvania—Philadelphia—Juvenile literature.
[1. Schenck, Charles—Trials, litigation, etc. 2. Freedom of speech. 3. Sedition.]
I. Title. II. Series.
KF4772.Z9A45   1999
342.73'0853—dc21   83-34010
                                              CIP
                                              AC

Printed in the United States of America

10 9 8 7 6 5 4 3 2

To Our Readers:
All Internet addresses in this book were active and appropriate when we went to press. Any
comments or suggestions can be sent by e-mail to Comments@enslow.com or to the address
on the back cover.

Photo Credits: Library of Congress, pp. 8, 28, 54, 63, 65, 87; National Archives,
pp. 20, 21, 23, 25, 34, 40, 43, 49, 58, 68, 80; Photo by Karen Alonso, p. 110.

Cover Photo: Corel Corporation

Contents

1

Assert Your Rights

On August 13, 1917, Charles Schenck pushed open the office door of the Socialist party's office at 1326 Arch Street in Philadelphia, Pennsylvania.[1] (Socialists believe that the work and wealth of a country should be divided among its citizens.) The meeting he was about to attend would change not only his life, but the lives of all Americans. As general secretary of Philadelphia's Socialist party, Schenck helped make decisions for his group. During the meeting, the party would decide how Philadelphia Socialists would respond to America's recent entry into World War I. Schenck and other Socialists opposed the new law that required men to register for the draft. The draft selected certain men, who then had to serve in the armed forces.

Charles Schenck and other members of the executive

committee voted to print fifteen thousand leaflets that spoke out against America's involvement in the war. They planned to send the leaflets to men who passed the test for military service. To accomplish this, the committee voted to give Schenck $125 for postage.

The leaflets were printed on both sides of the page. On one side, the heading read, "LONG LIVE THE CONSTITUTION OF THE UNITED STATES." On the other, the caption said, "ASSERT YOUR RIGHTS!" The leaflets stated that American involvement in World War I was only for the benefit of those who would make money from the conflict. They called the war a monstrous wrong against humanity that was committed by "Wall Street's chosen few." The leaflets urged the reader not to "submit to intimidation." According to Schenck's circulars, Americans should not be sent to foreign shores to shoot and kill the people of other lands.[2]

As a citizen, the leaflet argued, you violated the Constitution when you refused to recognize "your right to assert your opposition to the draft."[3] The leaflet's language became even more challenging: "If you do not assert and support your rights, you are helping to deny . . . rights which it is the solemn duty of all citizens and residents of the United States to retain."[4]

The leaflets compared military service to slavery,

which is prohibited by the Thirteenth Amendment to the United States Constitution. The most powerful statement in Schenck's circular said that a conscript, or drafted man, "was little better than a convict," because he lost his right to think and act as a free man.[5] The reader was urged to go to Socialist party headquarters and sign a petition to repeal the draft law.[6] Charles Schenck personally saw to it that the leaflets were printed and sent through the mail to conscripts.[7]

We do not know who it was, but someone did not like Schenck's message. We know this because Schenck was reported to the police. Charles Schenck was arrested for speaking out against the draft law. At the time of his arrest, the police found some of the leaflets piled on a table at the party's office at 1326 Arch Street. They also found some newspaper clippings containing lists of names and addresses of draftees. On September 15, 1917, Schenck was charged with violating a law that made it a crime to speak out against America's war effort. Essentially, Charles Schenck was arrested for saying what was on his mind. His fate would later be decided by a jury.

We know very little about Charles Schenck's personal life except for some of his political beliefs. Because there are no existing photographs of him, we do not even know what he looked like. But because he spoke

CELEBRATION OF THE ABOLITION OF SLAVERY IN THE DISTRICT OF COLUMBIA BY THE COLORED PEOPLE, IN WASHINGTON, APRIL 19, 1866.—[SKETCHED BY F. DIELMAN.]

Charles Schenck's antiwar leaflets compared military service to slavery. The Thirteenth Amendment to the United States Constitution outlawed slavery. This 1866 engraving from *Harper's* shows celebration among African Americans in Washington, D.C., following the passage of the amendment.

up about his beliefs, he affected the lives of every American for decades to come. It was Schenck's case that gave rise to the idea of freedom of speech as we know it today. However, the struggle for freedom of speech began long before Charles Schenck's journey through the American legal system. The fight for this constitutional right began even before America became a country. As you read about the history of this precious right, think about the many ways freedom of speech plays a part in your daily life.

2

America Claims the Right to Speak Freely

How many times each day do you voice your opinion? Think about the many times you have raised your hand in class to speak. You might have criticized your school's administration for rules you thought were unfair. You might even have signed a petition for a cause you supported.

From the very beginnings of this country, the right to free speech has been precious to Americans. Think again about the many ways in which you express yourself. What would happen if the law were suddenly changed? If you were no longer allowed to write a letter to the editor of your newspaper or to your representative in Congress, because you felt that some policy or law was unfair, how would you react? Would you, your friends, and parents protest such a law? With such a law, how *could* you protest?

Every time you give your opinion, you are using your right as an American citizen to freedom of speech. This right is guaranteed in the First Amendment to the United States Constitution. That amendment states: "Congress shall make no law . . . abridging the freedom of speech, or of the press." However, freedom of speech did not always exist in America and is found in few other countries in the world.

One reason that freedom of speech is so important to us is because it preserves the kind of country we want America to be. Every citizen who voices a belief helps shape the course of our nation's history. Another reason that the right to free speech is so important to Americans is because of the great cost of winning and keeping that right.

Development of the First Amendment

The struggle to win freedom of speech began even before our country became independent from England. The movement began with the case of John Peter Zenger in 1735. When Zenger was charged with the crime of criticizing the governor, America was still a British colony.

Since England was so far away from the American colonies, King George could not rule over the colonists effectively. Often, the king needed to make immediate decisions. For that reason, it was the custom to appoint a governor who would live in America and act on the king's behalf. Anyone who criticized the royal governor was seen as criticizing the king. Stirring up conflict in this way was known as the crime of seditious libel.

New York's royal governor in 1735 was William Cosby. Cosby was ill-tempered and interfered with the businesspeople and merchants of that time. For these reasons, many New Yorkers hated Cosby.[1] Frustrated business leaders in Colonial America decided to have a special newspaper called the *New York Weekly Journal* printed. The only purpose of that paper was to criticize the governor.

John Peter Zenger was the editor and printer of the *New York Weekly Journal.* In one of the issues, Zenger printed an article that challenged his government: "We see men's deeds destroyed, judges arbitrarily displaced, new courts erected, without consent of the legislature . . . trials by jury are taken away when a governor pleases."[2] Although Zenger did not personally write any of the articles, he was the one who was arrested. As the printer, Zenger was the only one to have his name appear on the newspaper.

Most colonists thought that the unfavorable statements in the newspaper about Cosby were true. Even so, Zenger was charged with seditious libel. According to English law in colonial times, seditious libel became a more serious crime when the criticism was based on fact. The reason for this situation was that a true statement was more likely to be believed. Therefore, the statements could cause more damage to the king's reputation.

Zenger asked for, and received, a trial by jury. However, his case was troubled from the start. His first lawyers had their licenses to practice law taken away simply because they agreed to defend Zenger. Yet two important points helped his case. The first was that the people on the jury hated Cosby. They also thought Zenger was a great hero because he dared to stand up to the difficult royal governor. The second point in Zenger's favor was that his new, secretly hired lawyer argued that defendants in libel cases should be found innocent if their statements were true.

Zenger's new lawyer asked the jury to ignore the law and consider the truth. He said:

> Men who injure and oppress the people . . . provoke them to cry out and complain; and then make that very complaint the foundation for new oppressions and persecutions. . . . [I]t is not the cause of a poor printer, nor of New York alone, which you are now

trying; No! . . . It is the best cause. It is the cause of liberty.[3]

Asking the jury to consider the truth instead of the law was an unusual argument in colonial days. However, the argument persuaded the jury to find Zenger not guilty of seditious libel.

With that jury verdict, American colonists began to win freedom of speech. This was not the only way that the colonists began to claim freedom. Less than fifty years after John Peter Zenger won his case, colonists won their independence from England. This began a new struggle as different ideas and values competed for recognition in the new country.

Separated from England, the various Colonial states came together in a loose association under the Articles of Confederation. Almost at once, Americans knew that the arrangement would not make America become the country they hoped to create. For instance, goods shipped from one state to another were taxed by each state through which they passed. This made commerce in early America clumsy and expensive.

A search for the solution to the problem was under way almost immediately. A new constitution, which would make the union of states much stronger, was proposed. It also gave the central, or federal, government a number of responsibilities and powers.

However, many of the Founding Fathers, like Thomas Jefferson, feared a strong central government.[4] Jefferson believed that having a federal government with too much power would be like having a king, with the same problems the colonists had hoped to eliminate with the revolution.

The answer seemed to be the Bill of Rights. This took the form of ten amendments to the United States Constitution. Each amendment limited the power of the central government. The first of these amendments guaranteed the freedom of speech that Americans had demonstrated was so important to them.

After long debate about the form that the amendment should take, the writers of the Bill of Rights included freedom of speech with other equally important rights like freedom of religion. The final language of the First Amendment to the United States Constitution specifically forbids Congress from "abridging the freedom of speech, or of the press. . . ."

The Founding Fathers made sure that freedom of speech was guaranteed in the Constitution. There was a widespread belief in the new country that such freedom was necessary if the new country was to survive.[5] Only unpopular ideas need protection. If the right to express an idea is kept out of politics, then there is less chance that the majority in the country will be able to suppress the minority. With the opportunity to voice ideas, comes the chance to change the popular point of view.

When the Bill of Rights was ratified in 1798, it became part of the United States Constitution. At that moment, the right to speak freely became a part of American history. Americans had won the right to free speech, but later it seemed that there were differing ideas about exactly what that meant.

Americans would argue over just how free speech should be. Throughout American history, Americans would even disagree over the definition of speech. However, it was not until World War I broke out that freedom of speech was tested in the United States Supreme Court.

3

The Road to Schenck

Starting in 1917, many changes occurred and new ideas emerged in the United States. Society itself was changing as labor unions began to gain power. (Unions are organized groups of workers. The main goal of a union is to improve the wages, hours, working conditions, and job security of its members.) Labor unions, like the Industrial Workers of the World (IWW), found conflict with other Americans in these passionate times. In Bisbee, Arizona, the sheriff and two thousand citizens took 1,186 IWW miners from their beds. They sent them by train to a New Mexico desert town, where they were left without enough food, water, and shelter for two days. Many Americans, including past president Theodore Roosevelt, thought this treatment of the union members was deserved.

Roosevelt explained that no human beings in their senses doubted that union members were determined to cause destruction.[1]

It was also a time of great anxiety, when communism triumphed over the established royal family of Russia. (Communism is a system of government that supports the ownership of all goods by all members of its society and does not recognize private property. The government in a Communist country controls production and distribution of goods.) The Russian Revolution made many Americans fear that such an event could happen in the United States. This concern was called the Red Scare, because Communists were known as Reds.

More troubling, World War I, the war between Germany and its enemies—England, France, and Russia—had finally drawn the United States into the conflict. Germany had warned the United States not to ship any supplies to its enemies. Any American ship found breaking this rule would be sunk by German submarines.[2] On May 7, 1915, the German threat became a reality. The luxurious ocean liner *Lusitania*, bound from New York to Liverpool, England, was attacked by the German Navy.[3] A single torpedo destroyed the ocean liner, sending 1,198 men, women, and children to their deaths. One hundred twenty-eight of those killed were Americans.[4]

Lieutenant Captain Karl Schweiger commanded the U-boat that sank the *Lusitania*. He recalled the event: "Many [life]boats crowded, come down bow first . . . and immediately fill and sink. . . . I cannot fire a second torpedo into this throng of humanity trying to save itself."[5]

Americans were outraged, claiming that sinking the *Lusitania* was "deliberate murder," and that Germans were "savages drunk with blood."[6] The nation braced for war, but Woodrow Wilson, then president of the United States, struggled to keep the nation out of the conflict. Three days after the *Lusitania* sank, Wilson said that "there is such a thing as a man being too proud to fight," and that America ought to stay out of the war.[7]

Unfortunately, American involvement in the war became inevitable. The German government tried to demand too many restrictions on American shipping. At last, even Wilson decided that there was no alternative other than war. On February 3, 1917, President Woodrow Wilson asked Congress to declare war on Germany.[8]

Wilson needed an army to fight the war, so he asked young men to enlist. The president called for some five hundred thousand men to volunteer for the Army. Only a few thousand responded to the call. The United

The ill-fated *Lusitania* is shown in the background, steaming out of New York Harbor. When a German submarine torpedoed and sank the ocean liner, many Americans demanded that the United States get involved in World War I.

States had never had to draft soldiers into service, but the unenthusiastic response to Wilson's call made drafting men into service necessary. On June 5, 1917, men between the ages of twenty-one and thirty were required to register for the draft and take tests to make sure they were fit for military service. If they passed, they had to join the military even if they believed that war was morally wrong. This process of gathering members of the military for service is called drafting, or conscripting.

Many men resisted the draft for a number of reasons. Some simply did not think that America

On February 3, 1917, President Woodrow Wilson stood before Congress to ask that war be declared on Germany.

should be involved in a war that really concerned only Europe.[9] Others objected to the war because of their religion or because they refused to be involved in any kind of violence. Some young men seemed to be pushed to extremes by fear of death on the battlefield. Two young men in Florida shot off parts of their arms to avoid military duty.[10] These people were called draft dodgers—people who refused to be drafted into military service.

Even people who would not be called up for service complained about the draft. A popular song during the beginning of the war was "I Didn't Raise My Boy to Be a Soldier." Kate O'Hare complained that the women of America were nothing more than "brood sows, to raise children to get into the army and be made into fertilizer."[11]

Patriots punished draft dodgers by dunking them in horse troughs, or painting them yellow—a symbol of cowardice. They also tarred and feathered those who refused to support the war, before driving them out of town.[12]

In all, more than 330,000 men either failed to register or ran away from the draft.[13] With so many avoiding service, the government had to do something to keep draft resisters from setting an example. If these men encouraged others to evade the draft, Congress

Charles Schenck and many other Americans objected to the policy that drafted men into the armed forces for service. President Wilson is being blindfolded before he draws the first number in the draft lottery.

feared it would not have enough soldiers to fight the war successfully.

To keep this from happening, Congress enacted the Espionage Act of 1917. Although espionage means spying, the law also made it a crime to interfere with United States involvement in the war. Therefore, the Espionage Act made it a crime to do anything that would encourage a drafted man not to report for military service. The law also made it a crime to encourage a soldier to refuse to do his duty. These crimes were felonies—the most serious level of crime that can be committed in the United States.

In case there were any war objectors who might fall between the cracks left in the Espionage Law, Congress later added other parts to the law. The new parts were known as the Sedition Act of 1918. Sedition means stirring up rebellion against the government. The Sedition Act gave the United States government almost unlimited power to examine any printed matter and keep it from being distributed. This is called censorship. The government could do this if it felt the information interfered with the war effort.

Anyone who violated this law could be fined up to ten thousand dollars and sentenced to twenty years in prison. The federal government arrested and tried two thousand people under this law. Nearly half were found guilty.

Hundreds of thousands of men either failed to register or left the country in order to avoid the draft. Women were not included in the draft system.

Some people were found guilty for doing things that might seem innocent. This was because almost anything that was critical of the war could be considered harmful to the war effort. For instance, the police in Minnesota arrested a man for telling a group of women that soldiers would never receive the socks the women were knitting.[14] Some people were imprisoned for criticizing the Red Cross and YMCA, organizations that helped soldiers.[15] People were punished for criticizing the government for selling war bonds or for saying that the war was against the teachings of Christ.[16]

Even something written in a personal letter could lead to a conviction for violating the Espionage Act. One person was convicted for writing: "I am for the people and the government is for profiteers."[17] One Montana man said that the flag was nothing more than a "piece of cloth with a little paint and marks in the corner."[18] He was arrested, convicted, and fined five hundred dollars, and he received a long prison sentence.

Even though many people avoided the draft, it was the popular opinion in 1917 that the United States was right to be involved in the war. Many Americans felt that all healthy young men ought to do their part by signing up for military duty.[19] Americans showed their support in various ways. Famous people like actor Douglas Fairbanks, Sr., and former president Theodore

Roosevelt encouraged other Americans to support the war. The American flag was displayed everywhere. Signs in shop windows encouraged citizens to buy war bonds to help pay for the cost of the war. Handheld traffic signs read on one side: "Go—Buy Bonds," and on the opposite side: "Stop—Buy Bonds."[20]

However, there were others, like Senator Bob La Follette, who did not agree that America should be involved in the war. La Follette was called a traitor for claiming this view.[21] Whatever their viewpoint, people on both sides of the issue spoke out. This conflict gave Americans the opportunity to explore the meaning of freedom of speech.

Masses Decision Brings New Ideas

When American courts began exploring the limits of the First Amendment's guarantee of freedom of speech, they first used the bad tendency test. Judges would ask whether a defendant's words had a bad tendency to lead to an evil that the government had a right to avoid. One such evil would be to interfere with America's participation in the war. Under the bad tendency test, the government could stop speech before it had an effect on its audience. For this reason, the bad tendency test was known as the nip-it-in-the-bud rule.[22]

The problem with the bad tendency test was that it

A Red Cross worker serves hot chocolate to an American soldier in France during World War I. One American was arrested for violation of the Sedition Act when he criticized the Red Cross, an organization that helped soldiers during the war.

could be used to include almost *any* kind of statement. A judge or jury could decide that any statement that criticized the government could have a bad tendency to interfere with the war's progress. Legal scholars like Zechariah Chafee and Judge Learned Hand began to question whether the bad tendency test conflicted with the United States Constitution. If almost any unpopular statement could be considered a bad tendency, then Americans really did not have the freedom to speak.

In 1917, Judge Learned Hand wrote a famous opinion in *Masses Pub. Co.* v. *Patten* that rejected the bad tendency test.[23] The opinion was written in a case decided in the Federal District Court for the Southern District of New York. Judge Hand's written opinion in the *Masses* decision led the way in opening up the right to freedom of speech. Later decisions would be influenced by Learned Hand's discussion of freedom of speech in the *Masses* opinion.

Masses Publishing Co., v. Patten

In July 1917 Patten, the postmaster of New York, refused to allow a certain newspaper to be sent through the mail. The newspaper was *The Masses*, a monthly revolutionary publication. Patten refused to send the paper through the mail because he determined that *The Masses* violated the Espionage Act of 1917. He said the paper "tended to produce a violation of the law . . . [by encouraging] the enemies of the United States, and to hamper the government in the conduct of the war."[24] The publisher of the newspaper sued to force the postmaster to send the monthly paper through the mail.

Patten objected to some cartoons and articles in the August 1917 issue of *The Masses*. One cartoon showed the Liberty Bell broken into pieces. Patten thought that the cartoon suggested the war had already destroyed the country's liberties.[25]

A second cartoon depicted a cannon. A young man is tied to the barrel of the cannon. A woman, marked "Democracy," is tied to the cannon's wheel, and a man, called "Labor," is tied to the cannon's carriage. A desperate-looking woman, marked "Motherhood," is kneeling on the ground next to her baby. According to Patten, the cartoon was meant to show that the draft destroyed youth, democracy, labor, and the family.[26]

Judge Hand wrote that it was not legal to "counsel or advise others to violate the law as it stands."[27] He said that political agitation, such as the cartoons in *The Masses*, may "stimulate men to the violation of the law."[28] However, Hand noted that each statement was "within the range of opinion and of criticism."[29] Rejecting the bad tendency test, Judge Hand suggested a test of his own: "[I]f one stops short of urging upon others that it is their duty or their interest to resist the law," then a court should not hold that the defendant tried to cause another to violate the law.[30]

The judge concluded that if his test was not used, then any political statement that stirs up dissent would be illegal.[31] Judge Hand was "confident that . . . Congress had no such revolutionary purpose in view."[32] Hand ordered the postmaster to deliver *The Masses* through the mail.

Later, Judge Hand's decision was overturned by the New York Court of Appeals, New York's highest court. Unfortunately, this case never reached the United States Supreme Court. However, Hand's decision in the *Masses* case was a turning point for freedom of speech in the United States. Judge Hand urged Supreme Court Justices like Oliver Wendell Holmes to reject the bad tendency test.

Several cases under the Sedition Act were being appealed to the Supreme Court. This would give the Court a chance to use a new test to decide whether certain speech was protected by the First Amendment. One of these cases was that of Charles Schenck. The United States would have to wait for the Supreme Court decisions in these cases to see whether Judge Hand's opinion in *The Masses* had influenced the Supreme Court.

Charles Schenck Tests Freedom of Speech

Schenck was an officer of Philadelphia's Socialist party. He believed, along with other members of his political party, that his organization should alert draft-age men about its feelings about being conscripted into service.

In order to spread its ideas, the Socialist party in Philadelphia decided to print fifteen thousand leaflets. The leaflets stated that United States involvement in World War I was brought about only for the benefit of those who would make money from the conflict. The leaflets urged the reader to "Assert your rights!"[33] Claiming that a drafted man was little better than a convict, Schenck's leaflet stated that United States citizens should not be sent to kill the people of other lands.[34]

Charles Schenck personally saw to the printing and distribution of these leaflets. Some of the papers were passed out by hand. Most were sent through the mail to men whose names appeared in the newspaper for passing the draft test. Since the leaflets made unfavorable comments about the war and the Army, Schenck was arrested for violating the Espionage Act.

Before a person accused of a serious crime goes to trial, the government must take steps to ensure that there is enough evidence to charge that person with one or more crimes. This process of officially charging someone with committing a crime is called an indictment. In order to indict a person, the government must present evidence, or information, to a grand jury. The members of the grand jury take an oath that they will fairly consider the evidence presented to them. The grand jury is not expected to decide whether or not a defendant is guilty. Its job is to decide whether there is enough evidence to prosecute a defendant.

In Charles Schenck's case, the government made three separate charges. The grand jury indicted Schenck on all three counts. Two of the charges of the indictment involved conspiracy to commit a crime. A conspiracy is the combination of two or more people who agree to commit a crime together. Charles Schenck was supposed to have conspired with Elizabeth Baer, another member of the Socialist party, to violate the Espionage Act. Baer was also arrested and charged with the crime of conspiracy. The last count against Schenck concerned an actual criminal act committed by Schenck.

Three Counts Against Schenck

The first count against Schenck was that he conspired, or worked with other people, to violate the Espionage Act. The subject of this count was that Schenck worked with Elizabeth Baer to produce the leaflet.

It was the government's position that the language in the flyer was meant to encourage the drafted men not

This truckload of men is under armed guard. They were found on the streets without their draft registration cards.

to appear for duty. Since Schenck supposedly worked with others to achieve this result, the government said he was guilty of conspiracy to cause disobedience in the armed forces.

The second charge leveled against Schenck was that he conspired with others to commit a crime against the United States. That crime was using the mail to send information that was not proper for mailing under the Espionage Act of 1917.

The third count charged that Schenck actually did use the United States Post Office to send material that was forbidden under the Espionage Act of 1917. In both the second and third counts, the materials that the government complained about were the leaflets printed by Schenck.

Charles Schenck was convicted of violating the Espionage Act and was sentenced to six months in jail. Schenck appealed his conviction because he believed the law violated his right to freedom of speech. The United States Court of Appeals agreed with the decision of the trial court and upheld the conviction. Since Schenck's defense involved a constitutional right, Schenck's appeal eventually reached the United States Supreme Court.

4

The Case for Charles Schenck

Two attorneys, Henry John Nelson and Henry J. Gibbons, brought Charles Schenck's case before the Supreme Court. The defense attorneys approached Schenck's defense in a very simple way. The defense really made only three points in its case. Two of the points concerned the government's evidence against Schenck. The last point raised was based on the First Amendment to the United States Constitution. All the arguments were explained to the Supreme Court in a document called a brief.

Schenck Questions the Evidence

Schenck's attorneys first questioned whether there was enough evidence to show that Schenck was involved in a conspiracy. Schenck said that there was not enough evidence to show that he conspired with anyone else to send the leaflets through the mail. According to the defense attorneys, the government had not proved its case. Therefore, Schenck's conviction should be overturned.

The second defense Gibbons and Nelson raised was whether the government should have been allowed to use certain evidence at Schenck's trial. The evidence Charles Schenck questioned was the leaflets taken by the police under a search warrant.

There is a strict set of rules that courts must follow. These rules are designed to make sure that no information is given to the jury to consider that might create a false impression. Only legally obtained evidence is admissible at trial.

Evidence that causes a defendant to testify against himself or herself at trial is not allowed. Charles Schenck believed the government used this type of evidence against him at trial. Schenck claimed that using the leaflets, for which he was responsible, was the same as making him testify against himself. The Fifth Amendment to the United States Constitution prohibits this. Schenck claimed that since the government violated this rule, his conviction should be overturned. He should be allowed to go free.

Gibbons and Nelson also questioned whether Schenck actually violated a law. The argument was more a matter of philosophy and emotions than a real legal defense. In their argument to the Supreme Court, the attorneys argued that Schenck was not a criminal

> . . . in the ordinary sense of the word. . . . This is a political question. No matter what the law may be, no matter what even this high court may decide, there is a question here of human freedom which will not down in spite of what the laws may say or what the laws may be.[1]

Then Schenck's attorneys pointed out that Schenck only spoke against the draft. According to the defense, Schenck did not urge anyone to avoid military service. Readers were responsible for the way they reacted to the leaflets. The men who received the leaflets could decide for themselves whether they would ignore Schenck's statements, or be persuaded, and avoid showing up for service.

Schenck's attorneys argued that "the right of free speech . . . gives the right to persuade another to violate a law, since, legally, it is actually the one who violates the law who should be punished."[2] If the drafted men agreed with Schenck's statements, and failed to show up for duty, they were the ones who interfered with the war effort. These were the men who should be prosecuted. Schenck's attorneys concluded this part of the argument

If a young man did not have a job that was essential to winning the war, he had to join the armed forces. Otherwise, he was labeled a *slacker*. Here a long line of slackers is being questioned.

by recalling an old saying: "You don't have to put your hand into the fire because I told you to do so."[3]

Schenck Raises the First Amendment Issue

Finally, Charles Schenck's attorneys raised their most important argument. They argued that the Espionage Law of 1917 violated the United States Constitution. Gibbons and Nelson said that the government's censorship of Schenck's leaflet kept him from sharing his opinion with other Americans. Schenck's right to freedom of speech, which is guaranteed by the First Amendment to the Constitution, had been violated. That amendment states: "Congress shall make no law . . . abridging the freedom of speech, or of the press."

According to the defense, this meant all Americans had the right to "absolutely unlimited discussion" of public matters.[4] This was the only way to "make sure that 'truth is mighty and will prevail.'"[5] Freedom of speech included Schenck's right to debate anything in which the government was involved. In their brief to the Supreme Court, Gibbons and Nelson asked, "How can the citizens find out whether or not a war is just or unjust unless there is free and full discussion!"[6] Then, the attorneys challenged the Supreme Court to consider the First Amendment issue. They asked: "Are we Americans big enough to allow honest criticism of the majority by the minority!"[7] Long ago, "it was held criminal to talk against flogging in the army; nowadays it is generally considered criminal to talk against Wall Street."[8]

If it was Schenck's opinion that the government was doing something that was wrong, Schenck should have the right to criticize the activity openly. As his attorneys asked the Court,

> How can a speaker or writer be said to be free to discuss the actions of the government if twenty years in prison stares them in the face if he makes a mistake and says too much? Severe punishment . . . will stop political discussion as effectively as censorship.[9]

Then, Gibbons and Nelson offered the Supreme Court their own version of a test to decide what kinds of speech should be protected by the First Amendment. "It would seem that the fair test . . . is whether expression is made with sincere purpose to communicate honest opinion or belief, or whether it does, in fact, incite to forbidden action."[10] Applying this test to the leaflets, the attorneys claimed that the circular did no more than call upon people to assert their constitutional rights.[11]

Finally, the defense argued that "[t]he worst that could be charged against the circular was that it said "a conscript [draftee] is little better than a convict.""

These men are being brought to an armory in New York City to be given the opportunity to explain why they were without draft registration cards.

Gibbons and Nelson pointed out that Congressman Champ Clark, speaker of the House of Representatives, used the same words in a speech to Congress. Although they did not specifically say so in their brief, the attorneys seemed to be wondering why this remark was acceptable for a Missouri congressman, but not for a political protester.

5

The Case for the United States

The government was concerned that if Americans were allowed to distribute information like that in Schenck's leaflet, many people might be persuaded that the United States should not be involved in the war. Many eligible men had already resisted the draft. If this trend continued, America's leaders feared they would not have enough eligible men to serve in the military. With too few soldiers, the United States could not possibly hope to fight the war successfully.

To protect the country's interests, the United States government prosecuted Charles Schenck for violating the Espionage Act—a federal crime. The attorney general's office represents the government in cases that appear before the Supreme Court. As special assistants to the attorney general, John Lord O'Brian and Alfred Bettman represented the government when Charles Schenck's case reached the Supreme Court.

Government Addresses First Amendment

The government attorneys claimed that the First Amendment had nothing to do with Schenck's case. They agreed with Schenck that the First Amendment protects "legitimate political agitation."[1] However, the attorneys argued, Schenck's leaflets went well beyond that boundary.[2] The government's brief to the Supreme Court pointed out that the leaflet was "full of bitter language against conscription." They reminded the Court of the leaflet's statement that "a conscript is little better than a convict."[3]

The government's brief did admit the leaflet contained an appeal for the repeal of the Selective Service Law—something that might be considered legal speech. However, Bettman and O'Brian argued that the statement was "not sufficiently strong to satisfy the defendant's purpose."[4] In order to satisfy their purpose, the government attorneys explained that Schenck's leaflets made a "frank, bitter, passionate appeal for resistance to the Selective Service Law."[5] Bettman and

O'Brian said that these words alone showed Schenck's criminal purpose to interfere with the draft.

The government attorneys claimed that there was more evidence that showed Schenck's criminal purpose. The fact that the leaflets were addressed to men who had already been drafted was important additional evidence.[6] Because the heading of the leaflet urged the readers to "Assert Your Rights," Schenck's purpose was clear to Bettman and O'Brian—rather than urging the readers to demand repeal of the draft law, it challenged conscripts to resist the draft law.

For these reasons, the government's brief claimed that Schenck's leaflet was not "speech" protected by the First Amendment, but an obvious attempt to encourage others to break the law by avoiding the draft—speech that is not protected by the First Amendment.

In any event, the government claimed the Supreme Court had already decided that the First Amendment was not involved in cases concerning the Selective Service Law—the law under which men were drafted for duty. These earlier cases were decided before the Espionage Law took effect. In those cases, the government lawyers reminded the Court, the Selective Service Law had been found constitutional. Therefore, any law made to prevent encouraging others to violate the draft law, like the Espionage Act, must be found constitutional.[7]

No Jurisdiction

The Supreme Court has the power to review certain categories of cases. This power is called subject matter jurisdiction. One kind of case the Court hears is appeals based on constitutional questions. Schenck's attorneys claimed that the Espionage Law violated their client's right to freedom of speech, which is guaranteed by the First Amendment to the United States Constitution. It was this claim involving the Constitution that allowed Schenck's case to be heard by the Supreme Court.

The government claimed that the constitutional question of freedom of speech was "too well settled" against Schenck. Because of the Selective Service Cases decisions, the constitutional claim in Schenck's case involving freedom of speech was not persuasive enough to give the Supreme Court jurisdiction.[8] According to the government, the case did not "genuinely and seriously" raise constitutional questions. Therefore, Schenck's case did not belong in the Supreme Court. The government brief recommended that the Supreme Court dismiss Schenck's appeal because the Court had no jurisdiction over the case.[9]

During this New York City slacker raid, soldiers stopped civilians (nonmilitary citizens) on the streets to make sure they had draft registration cards.

Government Answers Schenck's Other Claims

In its brief, the government responded to Schenck's claim that there was not enough evidence to prove that he was involved in a conspiracy to mail illegal literature. Bettman and O'Brian pointed out Schenck's admission that he was the general secretary of the Socialist party. As such, he was in charge of the headquarters from which the leaflets were sent.[10] It was noted that the general secretary's report stated that Schenck should be allowed some money in order to send the leaflets through the mail. According to the government, this was enough to prove that Charles Schenck was involved in a conspiracy.

Finally, the government attorneys answered Schenck's claim that the evidence used against him at trial was obtained in violation of the Fifth Amendment. Bettman and O'Brian replied that the leaflets and records were not taken directly from Schenck or from his home. The evidence was taken from the Socialist party's headquarters on Arch Street. The leaflets and records were not in the defendant's possession when they were taken by the police. Therefore, there could be no claim that there was a violation of the Fifth Amendment.

Both Charles Schenck and the United States government had made their arguments. The government argued the importance of national security and successfully fighting the war. Charles Schenck's argument was that the United States Constitution gave him the right to criticize the government. This included criticism of United States participation in World War I and criticism of the draft.

The Supreme Court was being asked to decide whether the ability of the United States to win the war was important enough to prevent Charles Schenck from speaking his mind. How would the Court resolve the conflict? Each interest was important, but it seemed that both interests could not exist at the same time. The nine Justices of the United States Supreme Court were left to consider the historic question of how free "free speech" ought to be.

6

The Decision

The landmark decision in the *Schenck* case was written by Justice Oliver Wendell Holmes. In years to come, Justice Holmes would be called the "champion of free speech and a free press."[1] However, it was not the *Schenck* decision that would earn this title for Holmes. It was over time that Justice Holmes explored the boundaries, and the need for protection, that the First Amendment required.

When Holmes wrote the *Schenck* opinion, he did so for a unanimous Court. All the Justices sitting on the Supreme Court agreed with the decision. Although the Court heard arguments from both sides in the case on January 9 and 10, 1919, the opinion was not handed down until March 3, 1919.[2]

Holmes Answers the Evidence Question

Holmes answered Schenck's Fifth Amendment argument very simply. He said only that the argument was "plainly unsound." The search of the Socialist party's headquarters had been performed with a valid search warrant. However, the Justice spent much more time discussing Schenck's claim that there was not enough evidence against him to show his involvement in any conspiracy, or that he was involved in sending the documents.

Justice Holmes pointed out that Charles Schenck was general secretary of the Socialist party. He was in charge of the headquarters building from which the documents were sent. Holmes then noted that according to the Socialist party's notes, Schenck personally saw to the printing of the leaflets. The same notes also showed that Schenck asked for, and received, money to pay for the postage to mail the flyers. For these reasons, Holmes said there was no doubt that Charles Schenck was involved in distributing the circulars. Finally, Justice Holmes turned to Schenck's First Amendment defense.

The First Amendment

Justice Holmes began his discussion of the First Amendment defense by admitting that Schenck's

Justice Oliver Wendell Holmes wrote the unanimous Supreme Court decision (against Charles Schenck) in the *Schenck* case.

argument was partly correct. Holmes said that in ordinary times, everything that Schenck printed in the leaflets would have been protected by the First Amendment. However, every act had to be considered according to the circumstances in which it occurred.[3]

Holmes gave an illustration to make his point clear. His example used a fictional man who falsely shouted "fire" in a theater. No matter how important Americans considered freedom of speech, such a statement would not be protected by the First Amendment. The result in such a case would be obvious. Needless panic and injury would follow such an irresponsible statement. In this case, the man's right to speak freely is not as important as public safety.

Holmes Announces a Test

Then Holmes wrote the words that made the *Schenck* decision one of the most well-known of all Supreme Court rulings: "The question in every case is whether the words used are used in such circumstances and are of such a nature as to create a clear and present danger that they will bring about the . . . evils that Congress has a right to prevent. It is a question of proximity and degree."

The "clear and present danger" test means that the government cannot punish a speaker until a real danger can be identified. The danger must be obvious and about to cause harm. Under Holmes's new test, a speaker could say more against the government than under the old bad tendency test. Under bad tendency, the government had to show little more than the simple possibility that the speech *might* cause some danger.

In order for a citizen to be punished under the clear and present danger test, Justice Holmes said that there must be a connection between speech and violation of a law. To be able to keep Schenck from mailing his leaflets, the Court had to find a connection between Schenck's speech and some illegal result. Justice Holmes and the rest of the Court decided that such a connection did exist between Schenck's leaflets and a harm that could result from the distribution of the material. After all, Holmes pointed out, "the document would not have been sent unless it had been intended to have some effect. . . ." The Supreme Court determined that Schenck expected to influence draftees to avoid serving in the Army.[4]

Again, the Court made the point that judgments depend on circumstances. "When a nation is at war, many things that might be said in time of peace are such a hindrance to its effort that [they] will not be endured so long as men fight. . . ."[5] The clear and present danger test was supposed to allow more antigovernment speech. However, Charles Schenck's leaflets were still considered too dangerous under the wartime circumstances.

Was Charles Schenck's "Attempt" Successful?

Finally, Holmes addressed Schenck's position on the effect his leaflets would have on draftees. Schenck seemed to admit that he should be punished for distributing the leaflets if the government could prove Schenck actually interfered with recruiting soldiers.[6]

However, the Court said that the Espionage Act punished more than actual interference with the draft. The act also prohibited conspiracies to obstruct the draft. Under the Espionage Act, the actual effect of the distributed leaflets was the same as the effect that Schenck intended to produce.[7] Schenck did not have to be successful to have committed a crime. The government simply had to show that Schenck's intent was to interfere with the draft.

The Supreme Court concluded under the clear and present danger standard that Schenck's leaflet *did* present a clear and present danger to the security of the United States. A unanimous Supreme Court upheld the decision of the lower court. Charles Schenck's conviction for speaking out against the draft had been confirmed by the "father of free speech."

Five thousand women tried to present an antidraft petition to the mayor of New York on June 16, 1917. The police ordered the women to leave. Three of the women were arrested when they attacked the police officers.

The Future of "Clear and Present Danger"

Holmes's new clear and present danger test was likely to be used in similar cases involving convictions under the Espionage Act. Even though Schenck's conviction was upheld, this new test sounded more demanding. The government should be required to show a greater connection between a defendant's speech and harm that the government is legitimately allowed to prevent. Did this mean that fewer examples of antigovernment speech would be found illegal under the Espionage Act? America did not have to wait long for an answer. On March 10, 1919, only one week after *Schenck* was decided, the Supreme Court handed down its decision in a case involving a popular American man of Schenck's time.

7

The Tide Begins to Turn

Announcing the "clear and present danger" test was only the beginning of the Supreme Court's exploration of freedom of speech. The test used in the *Schenck* decision was to be the subject of debate in the Supreme Court for decades to come. Justice Oliver Wendell Holmes gave the Court a new test but failed to explain some of the terms he used. How was a court to know whether a danger was "clear and present"? How far could a speaker go in criticizing the American government without being punished? Holmes gave little guidance in the *Schenck* decision.

Clearly, Justice Holmes favored more freedom of speech, but it would be a long time before the majority of the Supreme Court agreed with him. Finding the acceptable boundaries of antigovernment speech would take nearly half a century. The lengthy exploration could have been due to the fact that many Americans had mixed feelings about putting limits on speech. For example, the government publicly prosecuted Charles Schenck for speaking against the draft. However, private comments by the attorneys representing the United States suggested that they favored more freedom of speech.

Bettman told Congress that punishing a speaker for the tendency of what he said was contrary to the intent of the First Amendment.[1] O'Brian said that "freedom to express opinions, and in particular freedom to criticize are the phrases most important to us, because they provide . . . our democratic social structure."[2]

Although President Wilson led the nation in World War I, he seemed to share the prosecutors' mixed feelings about speaking against the draft. After the war ended, Wilson commuted, or changed, the punishments to ones that were less severe for more than one hundred convictions under the Espionage Act.[3] Over the course of other appeals based on the Espionage Act, the Supreme Court's decisions would reflect a similar struggle. Wherever the Court was heading in its examination of freedom of speech, Eugene Victor Debs directed its next step.

The *Debs* Decision

Eugene Debs was well known at the time of his arrest for violating the Espionage Act. He was very active in trying to get American workers to join unions in order to improve their pay and working conditions. Debs also ran for president of the United States four times as a Socialist. During the 1912 election, Debs received more than one million votes. He lost the election. However, almost one out of every one hundred Americans who voted in the election voted for him.[4]

Debs was opposed to America's involvement in World War I. On June 16, 1918, Debs gave a speech in Canton, Ohio, after visiting other socialists who had been jailed for giving antiwar speeches.[5] Eugene Debs believed that the jail sentence was a violation of their First Amendment right to freedom of speech. His speech focused mainly on socialism. However, Debs also took the opportunity to speak out against war. Debs said that the wealthy people in America declared war and that the working class fought the battles.

The "subject class," as Debs called the workers, had nothing to gain, and "everything to lose, including their lives," by fighting in the war.[6] Debs closed his speech by telling his audience they needed to know they were fit for "something better than slavery and cannon fodder."[7] Two weeks after giving this speech, Debs was arrested for

This Socialist antiwar meeting in New York on August 8, 1914, shows some of the many people who objected to American participation in the war.

violating the Espionage Act by interfering with the draft. After trial, he was sentenced to ten years in prison.[8]

Debs, like Schenck, appealed his conviction to the Supreme Court. Justice Holmes, once again writing the opinion of a unanimous court, made several observations. First, Holmes admitted that much of Debs's speech concerned the history and future of the Socialist party. That subject was not prohibited under the Espionage Act.[9] In fact, Debs's speech criticized war in general, without commenting on America's involvement in World War I.[10]

However, Debs did not have to directly encourage obstruction of the draft in order to violate the Espionage Act.[11] Debs told his audience that caution kept him from making known the extent of his opposition to the war.[12] Holmes claimed that Debs's audience would know he meant to show opposition to World War I. Holmes decided that "the natural and intended effect" of the speech would be to interfere with recruiting soldiers for the war.[13] The Supreme Court upheld the conviction of Eugene Debs for obstructing the recruiting service.

The phrase "natural and intended effect" was a retreat to the older attitude of the Court. This was more like the bad tendency test. Where was the clear and present danger test that Holmes had introduced only one short

Eugene Debs, Socialist and American presidential candidate is shown here. Debs was arrested and convicted under the same law as Charles Schenck.

week ago? Under clear and present danger, Debs might have had his conviction reversed. There was no indication that Debs's speech was likely to cause anyone to avoid the draft in any immediate way. Holmes's new test promised greater freedom in expressing opinions, but there was no evidence of that new test in the *Debs* decision. Would Holmes return to that new test? Once again, America would not have to wait long. The next step in exploring freedom of speech had its background in a revolution far from American shores.

Even as America and its allies fought in Europe during World War I, other historic events were taking place. For instance, Russia had suffered through a revolution. The new government declared that Russia would no longer participate in the World War. The United States did not support the newly self-appointed government and sent troops to the Russian port city of Vladivostok.

The *Abrams* Decision

In America, five young men resented America's military involvement with Russia's internal problems. All five were born in Russia but had lived in the United States for less than ten years.[14] They protested the invasion of Vladivostok by American troops and decided to take action.[15] One of those young men was Jacob Abrams.

Abrams and the others printed five thousand leaflets

in English and Yiddish—a language of European Jews and their descendants. The English leaflet said that President Wilson was a "coward" because he would not come right out and say that "[w]e capitalistic nations cannot afford to have a proletarian republic [a government made up of working-class citizens] in Russia." The leaflet written in English also included statements such as "Workers of the World! Awake! Rise! Put down your enemy and mine!"[16]

The Yiddish leaflet informed workers in ammunition factories that they were "producing bullets, bayonets, cannon, to murder not only the Germans, but also your dearest . . . who are in Russia and are fighting for freedom."[17] On August 22, 1918, Abrams and the other four men distributed the leaflets by throwing them from a factory window in New York City where one of the defendants was employed.

Abrams and the other four were arrested and charged with violation of the Espionage Act, the same law Schenck and Debs had been convicted of breaking. The specific charges stated that Abrams criticized the government at a time when the United States was at war with Germany. The prosecutor accused Abrams of making his statement with the intention of provoking resistance to the United States' involvement in World War I. The government also charged that Abrams urged

American soldiers are shown in Vladivostok, Siberia (Russia), on December 3, 1918. Jacob Abrams and other Russian immigrants in the United States objected to American "interference" and involvement in the Russian Revolution.

others not to produce the ammunition America needed in order to fight the war.[18] Abrams said he did not mean to cause harm to the United States and its involvement in World War I. He simply did not want American troops to interfere with the revolution in his homeland.

Abrams was found guilty and received a twenty-year prison sentence. He appealed, claiming that his actions were legal because the United States Constitution protected his freedom of speech. Abrams's attorney claimed that the Espionage Act was unconstitutional because it was in conflict with the First Amendment to the Constitution.

Supreme Court Justice John H. Clarke wrote the opinion for the majority of the Court. Justice Clarke rejected Abrams's claim that his speech was protected by the First Amendment. According to Clarke, this argument had already been used in the *Schenck* case, where the Court had decided that such speech was not protected by the First Amendment.

Justice Clarke also did not agree with Abrams's argument that he only intended to help the cause of the Russian Revolution. Clarke wrote that men must be "held to have intended, and to be accountable for, the effects which their acts were likely to produce."[19] Even if their main goal was to help the Russian Revolution, their plan would interfere with the United States' participation in World War I. Justice Clarke and the majority upheld Abrams's conviction.

This was the end of the story for Abrams and the other four young men. In a way, however, it was the beginning of the story for greater free speech rights for Americans. Justice Holmes wrote a dissenting opinion, with which Justice Louis Brandeis agreed. In a dissenting opinion, a Justice explains why he did not vote with the majority. In his dissent, Holmes used the clear and present danger test he mentioned in the *Schenck* opinion. This time, however, applying the test would bring very different results.

Holmes's Dissent in *Abrams*

Justice Holmes first pointed out that the Espionage Act required that the government must prove defendants *intended* to do damage to America's war effort.[20] Holmes believed that the government failed to do so in the *Abrams* case.[21] He wrote that it was very clear that the object of the leaflets was to "help Russia and stop American interference there against the popular government."[22] Holmes wrote that it may have been clear to Abrams and everyone else that his leaflets would hurt the war effort. However, unless Abrams printed and distributed the leaflets with the aim of hurting America's war effort, he could not be said to have done so with intent.

Then Holmes turned to the idea of freedom of speech. He wrote that Schenck and Debs were "rightly decided."[23] Holmes still believed that the United States could punish speech that is intended to produce "a clear and imminent danger" to the government.[24] Yet Congress should be allowed to limit freedom of speech only when there was a "present danger of immediate evil."[25]

Justice Holmes went further in expanding freedom of speech. He stated that "Congress certainly cannot forbid all effort to change the mind of the country."[26] Holmes wanted Americans to understand that knowledge is "imperfect." The best test of truth is the "power of the thought to get itself accepted in the competition of the market."[27]

Holmes said that Abrams's words were "a silly leaflet by an unknown man."[28] Therefore, no one could think that there was any danger that the words would have any effect on the country's efforts to win the war. Since that was the case, there was no "imminent" threat to America's involvement in the war. Justice Holmes completed his statements with a warning that Americans should always protect themselves against attempts to put limits on freedom of expression.[29]

Because Holmes's dissenting opinion was not the opinion of the Court, his opinion did not have the authority of law. However, his opinion was important for two reasons. First, Holmes added the "imminent harm" requirement to the "clear and present danger" test. If the Constitution ever adopted this standard, it would be more difficult for the government to prove a defendant's speech posed a threat to America.

Second, Justice Holmes's opinion supported the importance of exchanging ideas. It promised a new approach to the First Amendment's guarantee of freedom of speech—one that made greater allowances for the expression of ideas that did not agree with the majority of American citizens.

Eventually, Holmes's attitude toward freedom of expression would be the favored position. Later decisions of the Supreme Court would reflect the new idea. Before this would happen, however, the Supreme Court's freedom of speech decisions over the next fifty years would continue to wrestle with how much and how far people can go in self-expression. This struggle showed up in a series of Supreme Court decisions that seemed to swing back and forth between allowing free speech and prohibiting it.

DeJonge—The Fight Over Unions

In 1937 political conflict once again became the setting for exploring the boundaries of free speech. This time, instead of war, the tension was between the government and union organizers. Unions were being formed to give workers some power when dealing with their employers. Before union activity, those workers who complained about their pay or working conditions were simply fired. There were plenty of other workers ready to take the place of the "troublemakers."

When workers in a particular factory organized to form a union, they went on strike, or stopped working, if the employer ignored demands for better pay and conditions. Industrialists (people who owned or managed factories) felt as if they were losing control over their own property. As a result, states passed laws that made it a crime to use any unlawful act of force or violence as a way to bring ownership or control of industry under labor unions. This crime is called criminal syndicalism.

During a strike in Oregon in 1937, striking workers complained of raids on their homes. One of the striking dockworkers had also been shot by local police. The Communist party held a meeting for workers to discuss these concerns. During the meeting, no one suggested using any unlawful act to respond to the police or to employers' actions.[30] One man named Dirk DeJonge was arrested for helping to arrange the meeting. He was convicted of violating an Oregon law that made it a crime to arrange a meeting of any group that encourages criminal syndicalism.

The state court found that the Communist party had supported the use of criminal syndicalism at various times and places.[31] Even though no criminal activity was suggested at his meeting, DeJonge was convicted. Since the Communist party encouraged criminal syndicalism in general, it was against the law to arrange any meeting for its members. DeJonge's appeal eventually reached the United States Supreme Court.

The Court, through Chief Justice Charles Evans Hughes, stated that the First Amendment right to freedom of speech can be abused. However, the Court held that state laws are constitutional only when they prohibit that abuse. Speech itself cannot be prohibited. Therefore, holding a meeting where politics is discussed peacefully cannot be outlawed. The people who arrange the meetings cannot be branded as criminals.[32]

The Court decided that if the right to free speech was to be protected, laws could not control the organization that holds the meeting. Only the purpose of the meeting could be controlled.[33] If the purpose of DeJonge's meeting was peaceful discussion of the labor situation in Oregon, then he should be allowed to exercise his right to free speech.

The Supreme Court concluded that if members of

the meeting committed crimes at other times and places by urging violent responses to strikebreakers, then they should be punished for those actions. However, it is wrong to charge anyone with a crime for simply taking part in a peaceful assembly and discussion.

When *DeJonge* was decided, both communism and trade unions were still rather new concepts. Many state laws were passed to prevent or discourage membership in both types of organizations. Therefore, in *DeJonge*, the Supreme Court took a bold step forward in the history of freedom of speech. In the past, Supreme Court decisions had gone against the expression of dangerous ideas. Such ideas had a bad tendency to cause violent reactions. In *DeJonge*, the court allowed discussion of peaceful political action in a peaceful manner. Unfortunately for those who supported a liberal view of freedom of speech, the *DeJonge* decision did not signal a trend in allowing full freedom of expression. Only fourteen years later, the Supreme Court would address the issue of free speech again, and come to a very different conclusion.

The "Gravity of the Evil"

From 1945 to 1948, Eugene Dennis acted as one of the leaders of the Communist party in America. Dennis was convicted of violating the Smith Act. This law made it a crime to encourage, teach, or advocate the idea of destroying any part of the American government by force or by violence. At trial, the jury found that Dennis intended to overthrow the government "as speedily as circumstances would permit."[34]

Dennis complained that the Smith Act made it illegal even to have a conversation about Marxism or communism. This, Dennis argued, violated the very idea of freedom of speech. Chief Justice Fred Moore Vinson, writing for the majority of the Supreme Court in 1951, disagreed.

Vinson explained that the Smith Act prohibited individuals from urging overthrow of the government. The law did not prohibit discussion of the ideas the Communist party advocated. However, Vinson noted that Dennis's advocating the overthrow of the government by force or by violence contained an element of speech. For that reason, the Chief Justice believed it was necessary to examine the First Amendment to determine the boundaries of acceptable speech.[35]

Chief Justice Vinson wrote that the threat of violent overthrow of the government was certainly an important enough reason for the government to limit speech. He then examined the *Dennis* case, using a form of Holmes's clear and present danger test. Vinson adopted Judge Hand's rule that "in each case [courts] must ask whether the gravity of the 'evil,' taking into account the improbability of the plan, justifies invading free speech to the extent necessary to avoid the danger."[36] The Court decided that in this case, invading free speech was necessary to avoid the danger of revolution.

According to the Court, the clear and present danger requirement of the test did not demand much of the government. Certainly officials did not have to wait until the Communist party gave the signal to party members to begin an attack before the police could take action.

Chief Justice Vinson explained that it made no difference that the overthrow had not begun, and that it would probably not have succeeded if Dennis had tried to begin the revolt. Making an attempt to overthrow the government would cause a lot of damage.

Vinson recalled the jury's finding that the revolutionaries would try to overthrow the government "when they thought the time was ripe." He pointed out that the Communist party was a "highly organized conspiracy." World politics at the time were very uneasy, and the relations between the United States and Communist countries were of a "touch-and-go nature."[37] Vinson explained that the very existence of Dennis's group created the danger that the Smith Act tried to prevent. For these reasons, the Court upheld Dennis's conviction.

Eighteen years after the Supreme Court handed down its decision in *Dennis*, the Court would swing in the opposite direction. In 1969, the Court heard another freedom of speech case. Once again, the case dealt with issues loaded with emotional impact.

The Ku Klux Klan Holds a "Rally"

On a farm in Ohio, Clarence Brandenburg put on a white robe and red hood, and stood before a group of other people dressed in similar clothing. Brandenburg was one of the Ohio leaders of the Ku Klux Klan (KKK), a group that opposed equal treatment for minorities, especially African Americans and Jews.

Brandenburg had invited a local television crew to come and film the "rally" that the Klan was about to hold. The television crew filmed pictures of twelve people wearing the KKK robes. Some of the people at the rally carried guns. They gathered around a large wooden cross and set it on fire. During some parts of the film, the participants could be heard making racist and anti-Semitic (anti-Jewish) remarks.

Later in the film, Brandenburg made a speech in front of the camera. During that speech, Brandenburg made the following statements: "We're not a revengent [*sic*] organization, but if our President, our Congress, our Supreme Court, continues to suppress the white,

Caucasian race, it's possible that there might have to be some revengence [*sic*] taken."[38]

Clarence Brandenburg was arrested and brought to trial for breaking an Ohio law that made it a crime to encourage the use of violence and terrorism to cause political reform. He was found guilty, received a one thousand dollar fine, and was sentenced to prison for a term of no less than one year and no more than ten years.

Brandenburg appealed to the Supreme Court, claiming that the Ohio law violated his First Amendment right to freedom of speech. The decision in *Brandenburg* was written *per curiam,* Latin for "by the Court." The decision was written by the entire Court, instead of by one of the Justices.

The opinion of the Court included the test it used to decide whether Brandenburg's speech was protected by the First Amendment. The Court found that the constitutional guarantee of free speech means that a state cannot forbid support of the use of force. The only exception is a case in which the supporter intended to produce lawless action and was likely to succeed in producing such action.[39]

There are three obvious parts to the test used in the *Brandenburg* decision. The first requirement is that in order for speech to be controlled, the speech must be

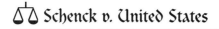

Even the most offensive, objectionable, and shocking statements are protected by the First Amendment, as long as the speaker is not trying to produce "imminent lawless action."

"directed to" producing lawless action. The government must show that the speaker meant for the audience to perform some lawless act in response to the speech. Otherwise, no criticism of the government would be allowed.

The second part of the *Brandenburg* test says that the lawless action must be imminent, likely to happen at any moment. If there is a long period between the proposed action and the time when the speech is made, the less likely it is for the act to take place. Listeners will lose interest, and other speakers will have a chance to suggest legal action.

Finally, the *Brandenburg* test requires that the advocacy of lawless action be likely to incite or produce such action. The right to discuss political ideas is very precious to Americans. Therefore, in political speech cases, the Court should demand near certainty that illegal acts will follow before speech is limited.

The Court also pointed out that in order to be constitutional, a law controlling speech must make a distinction between teaching the necessity of force and violence, and "preparing a group for violent action, and steeling it to such action."[40] Because the Ohio law did not make that distinction, the Court ruled the law unconstitutional. The Supreme Court unanimously reversed Clarence Brandenburg's conviction.

Brandenburg's words were offensive and shocking. However, the Supreme Court recognized that even members of the Ku Klux Klan had a First Amendment right to express their views.

Holmes's Test Modernized

Fifty years after Holmes wrote the *Schenck* opinion, the Supreme Court was still using a form of the clear and present danger test in *Brandenburg*. However, the more modern version of the test required that speakers intend to cause lawless action by their words and that they be likely to succeed. Holmes's test survived the passage of time. More important, his test was finally used not to suppress speech, but to enforce the constitutional rights of the speaker.

Each of the cases discussed so far involved people who gave their point of view through writing or speeches. Are speeches or written words the only way to make a political statement? Or can actions sometimes be a way of sending a message? The Supreme Court addressed these very questions.

8

Actions That Speak Louder Than Words

How people wear their hair, the type of music they listen to, the type of clothes they wear, and the religious and political beliefs they hold all say something about those people.

Making a "statement" may be something as simple as preferring rock music over jazz. It may be something as serious as protesting school officials searching through a student's locker. Buttons may be displayed to show the wearer's support for a political candidate or for philosophical ideas.

Sometimes, clothing can reflect a person's religious beliefs, as when a person of the Jewish faith wears a yarmulke (skullcap), or a Christian wears a cross.

Sometimes people wear special clothing to show pride in their ethnic backgrounds. Dashikis, kimonos, and kilts are worn by descendants of African nations, Japan, and Scotland, respectively, to show appreciation for the culture that is part of their background.

Are these choices merely actions, or are they statements? The answer to this question is important, because the First Amendment to the United States Constitution protects freedom of *speech*, not actions.

The Supreme Court had to answer this question when, more and more, protesters used actions instead of words to send their messages. In this chapter are the stories of several people who felt that their message would reach more listeners if they used actions to speak for them. The actions they made were symbols for the messages they wanted to send. Since their actions were often offensive, they hoped to get attention and spark conversation about their cause throughout the country. Whether this behavior was a speech instead of action, unprotected by the First Amendment, was something the Supreme Court had to decide.

Striking the Match That Sparked Conversation

In 1966, the United States was involved in a war in Vietnam. Participation in that war caused heated debate all over the country. Public protests and demonstrations against the war sometimes involved thousands of protesters. Violence broke out during many of these demonstrations as "peaceniks" confronted the police or National Guard. Several demonstrations were broken up by the National Guard, using tear gas. Nightly television news reports included scenes of these ugly events.

On one side of the debate were those who said Americans should support the government's decision to participate in the Vietnam conflict. Their motto was, My country, right or wrong.[1] On the other side were those who felt that war and violence were wrong, whatever the circumstances might be. Antiwar demonstrators marched into Washington, D.C., and other major cities by the tens of thousands. At times, the marchers chanted slogans directed to Lyndon Baines Johnson (LBJ), who was the president during part of the Vietnam War: "Hey! Hey! LBJ! How many kids did you kill today?"[2]

Much of the conflict centered on the fact that young American men were being drafted to serve in the armed forces. All American men over the age of eighteen were required to carry their registration certificate—or draft card—in their "personal possession at all times."[3] It was also a crime to change or destroy the card in any way.

David Paul O'Brien objected to the draft. To show

his opposition, O'Brien stood in front of the South Boston Courthouse and publicly burned his draft card. As he said later, he did it "so that other people would reevaluate their positions with Selective Service, with the armed forces, and reevaluate their place in the culture of today, to hopefully consider my position."[4]

O'Brien was arrested and convicted of burning his draft card in violation of the Universal Military Training and Service Act. He appealed to the Supreme Court, arguing that his act of burning the draft card was symbolic speech protected by the First Amendment. He claimed that the First Amendment guarantee of freedom of expression includes communicating ideas by conduct.[5] O'Brien claimed that his act was speech because he did it in "demonstration against the war and against the draft."[6]

Chief Justice Earl Warren, writing the opinion of the Court, disagreed. The majority of Justices acknowledged that symbolic acts could be considered speech, protected by the First Amendment. However, Warren wrote that he could not accept the view that an "apparently limitless" variety of conduct could be considered speech, simply because the speaker intends to express an idea.[7]

The Court decided that even if O'Brien's action could be considered speech, an important government

VALENTINE
DWORNIK
BORN 1949
DIED VIETNAM
1969

Moratorium -- October, November till the End of the War

PHOTO BY WINSTON VARGAS

The Vietnam War produced another wave of antiwar protests. This young woman is personalizing the loss of so many lives in Southeast Asia by displaying a picture of one of the soldiers who died in the line of duty. The armband the woman is wearing shows the number of soldiers who had died in Vietnam at the time the picture was taken.

interest could limit that speech. Chief Justice Warren created a test, later called the O'Brien Rule, to decide whether a law that limits speech is justified. The four parts of his test asked whether the law achieved the following:

- Is the law within the constitutional power of the government?

- Does the law support an important government interest?

- Is that interest unrelated to limiting free expression?

- Is the restriction on expression no more than necessary to achieve the government's interest?

The Supreme Court decided that the government had an interest in raising an army in a smooth and efficient manner.[8] The draft cards furthered this interest by making communication easier between the draft boards and the registered cardholder. The cards also made it easier for registrants to show that they were available to be drafted in a time of national crisis.

The Chief Justice wrote that the government interest was limited to keeping the selective service system running in a smooth and efficient manner. When O'Brien burned his card, he interfered with that important government interest. O'Brien was arrested for that alone. His arrest had nothing to do with the speech portion of his protest. For these reasons, the Supreme Court decided that the Universal Military Service and Training Act was constitutional, and it upheld O'Brien's conviction. In the meantime, however, the Supreme Court recognized that certain actions could be considered speech worthy of First Amendment protection.

Almost twenty years later, another young man would set fire to an object on the steps of a courthouse. This time, the protest was not about a foreign war, but an attempt to communicate his ideas about America's political situation. The result of the following case would expand the definition of symbolic speech even further.

Burning the Flag

A presidential election was held in the United States in 1984. The Republican party had renominated President Ronald Reagan to run as their candidate. Gregory Lee "Joey" Johnson was a member of the Revolutionary Communist Youth Brigade. This group opposed Reagan's renomination, and saw the American flag as a symbol of international oppression.[9]

During a public protest, Johnson accepted a stolen American flag from a fellow protester, as they marched through the streets of Dallas, Texas. The march ended on the front steps of Dallas City Hall. There, Johnson opened up the flag, soaked it in kerosene, and set it on fire. While the flag burned, the protesters chanted "America, the red, white, and blue, we spit on you."[10]

Johnson was arrested, not for his message, but for the way he delivered it. By burning the flag, he broke a Texas law against "Desecration of a Venerated Object."[11] The law prohibited damaging or mistreating the national flag in a way that the offender knew would "seriously offend one or more persons likely to observe . . . his action."[12]

At Johnson's trial, the prosecutor said that Johnson posed a danger to Texas by "what he does and the way he thinks."[13] Several witnesses testified that they had been seriously offended by the flag burning. Daniel Walker was one of those witnesses. After the demonstration was over, Walker collected the remains of the flag and buried it in his backyard.[14] Johnson was found guilty and was sentenced to one year in prison. He was also fined two thousand dollars. Johnson appealed to the Texas Court of Criminal Appeals, claiming that his actions were protected by the First Amendment as symbolic political speech. The court of criminal appeals agreed with Johnson's argument, and reversed his conviction. The state of Texas appealed to the United States Supreme Court, asking that the conviction be reinstated.

The state of Texas argued to the Supreme Court that it had two important interests to preserve. First, the state had an interest in preventing the breach of the peace that flag burning could produce. The state also said it had an interest in preserving the flag as a symbol of "national unity."[15] Texas prosecutors claimed that burning the flag would cast doubt on whether national unity actually existed. They said that "if a symbol over a period of time is ignored or abused, it can . . . lose its symbolic effect." Therefore, the state held that Johnson's message was a harmful one that should not be allowed. The state admitted that it might not be able to prevent words or acts critical of the flag. At the very least, the prosecutors argued, they should be able to prevent "outright destruction of the flag."

Joey Johnson argued simply that burning the flag was symbolic speech, protected by the First Amendment. Therefore, Johnson's attorneys said that the decision of the Texas Court of Criminal Appeals, reversing his conviction, should be upheld by the Supreme Court.

In a 5-4 decision, Justice William Brennan wrote the opinion for the majority of the Court. In the beginning of his opinion, he questioned the state's two main arguments. First, Brennan noted that there had been no breach of the peace after Johnson burned the flag, and that there was only an "assumption" that the act would provoke violence. The assumption was not enough to allow the government to prevent Johnson from speaking.

Brennan next wrote about Texas's interest in preserving the flag as a national symbol. In response to that argument, the Justice wrote that "if there is a bedrock principle underlying the First Amendment, it is that the government may not prohibit the expression of an idea simply because society finds the idea itself offensive or disagreeable."[16]

Justice Brennan pointed out that if a law allowed burning a flag when it became too dirty or old to be a proper national symbol, but forbade flag burning as a way to show contempt for the flag as a symbol, the law would be allowing the flag to be used as a symbol "only in one direction."[17] Brennan claimed that this would lead to the law imposing one set of preferences on the people of the country, something that the First Amendment itself forbids.[18]

Justice Brennan admitted that the American flag was an important national symbol and that the government had an interest in encouraging proper treatment of the flag. However, criminally punishing a person for burning a flag as a means of political protest was not an acceptable way to encourage respect for the nation's symbol.

At the end of the opinion, Justice Brennan wrote: "We can imagine no more appropriate response for burning a flag than waving one's own, no better way to counter a flag burner's message than by saluting the flag that burns. . . ."[19]

Brennan stated that we should not honor the flag by punishing its destruction because that would weaken the freedom that our national symbol represents.[20]

The Supreme Court agreed with the court of appeals that Johnson's conviction should be reversed. The Supreme Court ruled that burning the American flag as a political protest was speech, and therefore, protected by the First Amendment to the Constitution. However, far from settling the debate about flag burning, the Court's *Johnson* decision simply touched off angry conversation across the United States.

Congress, then-President George Bush, and ordinary American citizens, all joined in angry protest over this decision. The protest would burn more brightly than Johnson's stolen flag. Even after Congress acted and the Supreme Court responded, the discussion continued.

Congress Passes the Flag Protection Act of 1989

Many Americans expressed their outrage over the Supreme Court's decision in *Johnson*. Congress

93

disagreed with the Court's decision, and promised to find a way to punish those who burned the flag.

Some Americans, like President Bush, wanted to amend the Constitution to make it a federal crime to burn the flag. They feared that a federal law would be struck down by the Supreme Court, just as the Texas law had been.[21] However, members of Congress believed they could write a law that would be upheld by the Supreme Court.

The challenge was to write a law that did not mention any message meant to be sent by a flag burner. If the law focused simply on the act of burning the American flag, then the Supreme Court could not rule that the law was designed to suppress any point of view.

Congress set about this task, and the result was passage of the Flag Protection Act of 1989 by an overwhelming vote. The new law made it a crime to deliberately burn, deface, or trample on the American flag. Anyone who mistreated the flag could be fined and sent to prison for one year. The law made an exception for those people who wanted to dispose of a worn or soiled flag. One person immediately broke the new law in order to test its constitutionality. Once again, the question of flag burning was brought before the Supreme Court.

The *Eichman* Case

The case against Shawn Eichman was dismissed at trial, because the United States District Court for the District of Columbia found the 1989 law to be unconstitutional. Federal prosecutors appealed, asking that the Flag Protection Act be upheld, because it was different enough from the law involved in the *Johnson* case to be found constitutional. The government pointed out that the new law did not mention the flag burner's "motive, his intended message, or the likely effects of his conduct on onlookers."[22]

Once again, the Supreme Court delivered a 5-4 decision, in an opinion written by Justice Brennan. Brennan wrote that the law did not mention any limits on flag burning because of the protester's message. However, it was clear to Brennan and four other Justices of the Supreme Court that the government's interest was connected to limiting freedom of expression.

The Court's opinion pointed out that the language of the law showed that the government was interested in the message carried by the act of flag burning. All the terms used in the language of the act concern disrespectful treatment of the flag. Therefore, the law still suppressed freedom of speech out of concern for the message being sent. According to a majority of the Supreme Court, this intent to prohibit speech because of its content made the Flag Protection Act of 1989 the same as the Texas law in *Johnson*. The Supreme Court affirmed the decision of the lower court, holding that the Flag Protection Act unconstitutionally suppressed freedom of speech.

Burning the American flag is a very deliberate way to send a message. Yet the Supreme Court decided that such an act should be protected by the First Amendment. If flag burning is legal, then it is difficult to imagine that any sort of statement would be found offensive enough to suppress. Yet a number of limits on speech still exist. The following chapter of this book describes those limits.

9

Limits on Free Speech

The cases that grew out of the protest against war and a presidential election opened the door to further debate about the First Amendment. The reason for freedom of expression is no less than the need to exchange ideas freely. It is this free exchange of ideas and information that leads to finding the truth. However, there is a need for some limits. We live in a society, so we should be aware of others' sensitivities. We also live under a form of government that sometimes must limit speech. Sometimes a government has needs that can conflict with an individual's need to speak. The Supreme Court has developed a number of ways to determine whether limits to speech are acceptable. Tests help the Court decide whether the society's interest or the individual's right to speak should prevail.

We have already seen one such test—clear and present danger—at work in the many cases from *Schenck* to *Brandenburg*. In some cases, the nation's interests prevailed over the individual's right to speak out. In more modern times, however, the individual's right to speak is being enforced even when the speaker's message is offensive to others. Even though individual rights seem to be valued more and more, a form of the clear and present danger test still remains one way in which the Court can limit speech.

The Supreme Court has also upheld some state and local laws that limit speech in some way. These rules are called "time, place, and manner restrictions." The restrictions on speech are allowed only if the laws reasonably affect the way in which the message is delivered—not the message itself. The general rules developed by the Court to make these restrictions permissible are the following:

- The restrictions must have nothing to do with the content of the speech. For instance, a city law that prohibited all billboards—not just some categories— would be allowed by the Supreme Court, since the obvious intent of the law is to keep billboards from cluttering a town, not to suppress speech.

- The restriction cannot restrict more speech than is necessary to serve the government's important interest. For instance, a city law might require any group using the city theater to use the city's sound system. The city has an important interest in controlling noise. At the same time, this law does not keep the performers from sending their "message," and it does not create a serious burden.[1] Other important government interests are litter control, personal privacy, and traffic safety.

- There must be other, reasonable ways for the speaker to deliver the message. For instance, a city law that prevented targeted picketing—picketing in front of a single home—was upheld. The Supreme Court found that other means to deliver the message were available, because the protesters could have marched through the neighborhood.[2]

Many questions remain unanswered. One such question is whether the right to speak freely exists in special places like schools, where authorities have a special responsibility to keep an orderly atmosphere. Once again, America's involvement in the Vietnam War would provide the spark for the discussion.

Mary Beth Tinker's Silent Protest

College-aged American men were drafted to take part in the Vietnam War. Many students became very vocal about their opposition to the war. Others found quiet ways to show they did not support the war in Vietnam.

Mary Beth Tinker was one of those protesters. In December 1965, she and a group of other high school students in Des Moines, Iowa, devised a creative way to show their objection to the war. Instead of using their voices, these students "spoke" with their actions. Mary Beth Tinker and her friends decided to wear black armbands to school during the holiday season that year.[3]

Black armbands are traditionally worn to show grief over a death. Therefore, wearing the armbands during the holidays would be a constant reminder of the deaths of American servicemen in Vietnam. When the school officials learned of the plan, they announced that this demonstration would not be allowed. They said that any student who came to school wearing a black armband would be suspended until the band was removed.[4]

Mary Beth and several other students ignored the warning and wore the armbands to school. When they were suspended, they filed suit in federal district court to keep the school officials from preventing their return to school.

The district court held that the school officials' actions were reasonable, because it was part of their job to keep peace and order in the school. If some students were allowed to make this protest, it would cause disruption in the classroom.

Mary Beth and the other students appealed to the court of appeals and finally to the Supreme Court, saying that this form of protest was "speech" protected by the First Amendment to the United States Constitution. Justice Abe Fortas, writing for the majority of the Supreme Court, agreed. He wrote that First Amendment rights are "available to teachers and students." Fortas noted that "students do not shed their Constitutional rights to freedom of expression at the schoolhouse gate."

The opinion stated that school officials tried to punish Mary Beth Tinker for her point of view. Her form of protest was not disruptive and caused no interference in the school. Because she caused no disturbance, there was no need for school officials to prohibit her from using this form of protest.

The Supreme Court agreed with the district court that school officials had to control behavior in their schools. However, the simple concern that a disturbance will result from a protest is not enough to take away a student's right to freedom of expression. The school should also be required to show that not allowing students to wear armbands is caused by more than a desire to avoid the unpleasantness that "always accompanies an unpopular viewpoint."[5] Fortas said that the officials had to show that Mary Beth Tinker's silent protest would "materially and substantially interfere with . . . appropriate discipline in the operation of the school."[6]

As with Justice Holmes's clear and present danger test from *Schenck* fifty years earlier, Justice Fortas used a test to decide whether school officials could keep Mary Beth Tinker from expressing her point of view. Both this test and the clear and present danger test required showing that the behavior or speech threatened to cause some kind of serious harm before that speech could be prohibited.

Even in a special place like a school, where authorities had a responsibility to keep order, students had the right to express their points of view. Only when the protest interfered with the purpose of that special place could the government interfere.

Clearly, the Supreme Court's recent decisions were broadening free speech rights in America. Do these decisions of the Court mean that an American wishing to speak out can make any statement, using any sort of vocabulary? The answer is that it all depends on the facts of the case. The Court has spent years developing the boundaries of acceptable speech.

Speech That Is Not Protected

There are some categories of speech that the Court has prohibited. This is speech that has nothing to do with an exchange of ideas. In these cases, the speaker only attempts to provoke the listener. Therefore, speech in certain categories receives no First Amendment protection. These categories are not mere "time, place, and manner" limits on speech. At times, even the message must be restricted. The value of this kind of speech is so low that the interest of keeping order and morality becomes more important than freedom of expression.

"Fighting Words"

One category of speech that is not protected is that of fighting words. This type of speech was addressed by the Supreme Court in 1946. A man named Chaplinsky, a Jehovah's Witness, spoke out on a public street, claiming to passers-by that all organized religions were a racket. When the gathering crowd became restless, a disturbance broke out, and Chaplinsky was arrested.

Chaplinsky argued with the arresting officer and called him a "damned Fascist." Fascism is a system of government noted for the overbearing and warlike ways of its leaders. Chaplinsky's words to the officer led to his conviction for violating a law against calling any other person by an offensive name. Was it Chaplinsky's right to voice his opinion about the officer? Did New Hampshire's law prohibiting the use of offensive names diminish the First Amendment's protection?

The Supreme Court answered no to these questions in an opinion written by Justice Murphy. He wrote: "It is well understood that the right of free speech is not absolute at all times and under all circumstances."[7] According to Murphy, there are certain classes of speech that have never been thought to raise any constitutional problem. "These include the . . . obscene . . . and . . . insulting or 'fighting' words."[8] The Justice defined fighting words as those that inflict injury simply by being spoken, or "tend to incite an immediate breach of the peace."[9] Such words have nothing to do with explaining an idea, and have slight, if any, social value. Justice Murphy and the majority of the Court affirmed Chaplinsky's conviction, stating that "personal abuse is not in any proper sense communication of information or opinion safeguarded by the Constitution."

Obscenity

Another class of speech that has traditionally not been protected by the First Amendment is obscenity. It has been defined by the Supreme Court as a description of sexual conduct that the average person in a community would feel appeals to a shameful interest in sex in an offensive way.[10] The Court has also found that in order to be considered obscene, the material must have no serious literary, artistic, social, or political value.[11]

However, the Court has sometimes made exceptions to the rules on fighting words and obscenity, stating that the speech must be considered in context. For instance, calling another person a Fascist to his face could be considered fighting words, and therefore, not protected by the First Amendment. However, this was held to be protected speech in a case involving a striking worker. The Court said that it was to be expected in the "give and take of . . . economic" disputes.[12]

In much the same way, four-letter words are ordinarily considered obscene. However, there are exceptions. In 1971 an obscene word written on the back of a young man's jacket was held to be protected speech. That word was used in connection to the draft during the Vietnam War. The Supreme Court ruled that the obscene term was not directed personally to those who might read the message on the jacket, however offended they might be.[13]

Freedom of Speech—Still Protected

Over the course of almost eighty years the Supreme Court made a dramatic change in its rulings on First Amendment cases. At first, statements that criticized the government were punished. However, Justice Holmes pointed the Court in the direction of expanding freedom of expression.

Today, it seems that there are fewer limits on free speech. Some remaining limits have weakened, as each statement must be considered in context. Americans have certainly won the First Amendment right to freedom of speech through the years. Decide for yourself whether the extent to which we enjoy freedom of expression today was intended by the Founding Fathers.

10

The Future of Freedom of Speech

The concept of freedom of speech has provided the subject for lively debate throughout American history. Over the course of eighty years, the Supreme Court addressed many issues concerning freedom of expression. These issues ranged from questions on whether or not American citizens can criticize the government for participating in a war to whether or not an individual can burn the American flag as a form of protest. The Court has even addressed the question of whether the government can punish the use of obscenity, when it is used to demonstrate the extent of a protester's anger.

Because the Court has answered so many questions about how Americans can voice their objections, and express their ideas, it may seem that no open questions on the subject remain. However, questions still arise, on a daily basis. For instance, should the government be able to censor or control a famous musician's song lyrics, when the words to the song celebrate the murder of a police officer?

Freedom of speech affects almost every aspect of life. The topic even enters into the advertisements read in public. In 1997, New York City's Metropolitan Transit Authority (MTA) announced new rules on the subjects that could appear in its subway advertisements. The MTA was concerned about advertisements that might be offensive to the public that used the subways, buses, and trains.[1] Past ads had shown minors in sexually suggestive poses. Others were violent or offensive to a large segment of the public in some other way. The MTA's announcement sparked yet another discussion on freedom of speech.

One critic of the new rule said that the "MTA is not permitted to accept or reject an ad on the basis of the viewpoint . . . in the ad." The critic feared that the MTA's rule would "open the door to censorship of political advertising on buses and trains."[2] One New York City assemblyman said that MTA standards "went against . . . [the] city's long history of lively debate."[3]

Other New Yorkers supported the rules, claiming

that "there's no question that there are parents . . . who will not allow their children to ride in the subway, in part because of the ads."[4] Where will the debate end? It is difficult to say, because advertisers have the right to express their views in advertisements. However, the public also has the right to use public transportation without being exposed to obscenity or to some other forms of offensive speech.

One judge's recent sentence of a criminal defendant also raises First Amendment issues. Luis Felipe, leader of The Latin Kings, a New York City gang, was sent to prison in 1991 for possession of stolen property. While he was in prison, trouble arose within his gang, as members tried to gain control of the organization. From his prison cell, Felipe ordered the execution of the disloyal gang members. Three Latin King members were murdered at Felipe's order.

As a result, Judge John Martin sentenced Felipe to life imprisonment plus forty-five years. The judge ordered that Felipe would serve the entire sentence in solitary confinement, allowed to speak only to his lawyer and close family members. Luis Felipe has no close relatives.[5] The judge found that the strict measures were necessary to keep the gang leader from ordering executions from his jail cell.[6]

Luis Felipe responded to the judge's sentence: "You

Freedom of speech protects a person's right to express ideas and opinions. Does that mean that graffiti is protected by the First Amendment? Is there a "legitimate government interest" that would allow the government to punish this "speech?"

sentenced me to die day by day. . . . I don't mind my mail to be monitored, but you are telling me nobody can write to me . . . nobody can care about me [any] more?"[7] The judge even refused Felipe's request to write to a prisoner's rights group.

Luis Felipe's story raises the question of how the government can punish a prisoner, but it brings up First Amendment questions as well. Can the government prevent a convict from talking to friends or even to organizations that may help his legal situation? Judge Martin found that the restrictions were necessary to keep Felipe from ordering more executions from jail. Was there another, less restrictive way that officials could monitor Felipe's messages without completely taking away his First Amendment rights?

Luis Felipe and advertisers in the MTA system may eventually reach the Supreme Court with their questions. Both stories demonstrate the fact that each freedom of speech problem poses a difficult task for judges. Both sides have strong arguments in their favor. It is this friction that will continue to bring free speech cases to the Supreme Court. As First Amendment stories unfold in the newspapers, you can follow their progress through the courts. In this way, you can become part of the national conversation and use the constitutional right that makes our country so special.

Questions for Discussion

1. The clear and present danger test is more than seventy years old. Look at the more recent cases discussed in this book, like the flag-burning cases. Would the clear and present danger standard work today? Explain your answer.

2. Look at the test proposed by Schenck's attorneys again. It's in Chapter 4, "The Case for Charles Schenck." Do you think Schenck should have been convicted or freed if that test were used by the Supreme Court? Why?

3. A congressman also made the comment that a conscript was "little better than a convict." Could he have been convicted under the clear and present danger test? What might he have been referring to? Would his intent have made any difference under the test? What if he was trying to get better supplies for soldiers?

4. Schenck's leaflet never specifically told the reader to avoid the draft. However, Justice Holmes stated that the leaflet "would not have been sent unless it had been intended to have some effect," namely, the obstruction of the draft. Could Schenck have included any other statements in the leaflet that would have changed Holmes's mind? *Should*

Schenck have had to satisfy Holmes's concerns about the possible effects of the leaflets on the readers?

5. Look around the walls and fences of your hometown. Are any of them covered with graffiti? Are the comments and drawings that make up the graffiti a kind of speech that is protected by the First Amendment? Write down how you reached your decision.

Chapter Notes

Chapter 1. Assert Your Rights

1. *Schenck* v. *United States*, 249 U.S. 47, 49 (1919).
2. Ibid., p. 51.
3. Ibid.
4. Ibid.
5. Ibid., pp. 50–51.
6. Ibid., p. 51.
7. Ibid., p. 49.

Chapter 2. America Claims the Right to Speak Freely

1. Robert J. Wagman, *The First Amendment Book* (New York: Pharos Books, 1991), pp. 144–145.
2. David Colbert, ed., *Eyewitness to America* (New York: Pantheon Books, 1997), p. 41.
3. Ibid., pp. 43–44.
4. John Mack Faragher, ed., *The Encyclopedia of Colonial and Revolutionary America* (New York: Da Capo Press, 1996), p. 215.
5. Wagman, p. 1.

Chapter 3. The Road to *Schenck*

1. Robert H. Ferrell, *Woodrow Wilson and World War I* (New York: Harper and Row Publishers, 1985), p. 209.
2. Howard Zinn, *A People's History of the United States* (New York: HarperPerennial, 1995), p. 352.
3. Ferrell, p. 10.
4. Ibid.

5. Irving Werstein, *Over Here and Over There* (New York: W. W. Norton & Company, Inc., 1968), p. 73.

6. Roger Butterfield, *The American Past* (New York: Simon & Schuster, 1957), p. 353.

7. Ferrell, p. 10.

8. Werstein, p. 126.

9. Zinn, p. 361.

10. Ibid.

11. Ibid., p. 363.

12. Ibid., p. 204.

13. Ibid., p. 361.

14. J. Edward Evans, *Freedom of Speech* (Minneapolis, Minn.: Lerner Publications Company, 1990), p. 34.

15. Thomas L. Tedford, *Freedom of Speech in the United States* (New York: McGraw Hill, Inc., 1993), p. 51.

16. Zechariah Chafee, Jr., *Free Speech in the United States* (Cambridge, Mass.: Harvard University Press, 1941), pp. 39–40.

17. Tedford, pp. 50–51.

18. Ferrell, p. 204.

19. Evans, p. 33.

20. Ferrell, p. 203.

21. Werstein, p. 174.

22. Tedford, p. 54.

23. *Masses Publishing Co.* v. *Patten* 244 F. 525 (2d Cir.) 1917.

24. Ibid., p. 536.

25. Ibid.

26. Ibid.

27. Ibid., p. 540.

28. Ibid.

29. Ibid., p. 539.

30. Ibid.

31. Ibid., p. 540.

32. Ibid.

33. *Schenck* v. *United States*, 249 U.S. 47, 51 (1919).

34. Ibid.

Chapter 4. The Case for Charles Schenck

1. *Schenck* v. *United States*, 249 U.S. 47 (1919), Brief for Schenck, p. 31.

2. Ibid., p. 7.

3. Ibid.

4. Ibid.

5. Ibid.

6. Ibid., p. 8.

7. Ibid.

8. Ibid.

9. Ibid., p. 6.

10. Ibid., p. 14.

11. Ibid.

Chapter 5. The Case for the United States

1. *Schenck* v. *United States*, 249 U.S. 47 (1919), Brief for the United States Government, p. 13.

2. David M. Rabban, *The Emergence of Modern First Amendment Doctrine* (Chicago: University of Chicago Law Review, 1983), vol. 50, no. 4, p. 1255.

3. *Schenck* v. *United States*, Brief for the United States Government, p. 13.

4. Ibid.

5. Ibid.

6. Ibid.

7. Rabban, p. 1252.

8. *Sugarman* v. *United States*, 249 U.S. 182 (1919).

9. *Schenck* v. *United States*, Brief for the United States Government, pp. 20–21.

10. *Schenck* v. *United States*, 249 U.S. 47, 49 (1919).

Chapter 6. The Decision

1. Robert J. Wagman, *The First Amendment Book* (New York: Pharos Books, 1991), p. 57.

2. *Schenck* v. *United States* 249 U.S. 47 (1919).

3. Ibid., p. 52.

4. Ibid., p. 51.

5. Ibid., p. 52.

6. Ibid., p. 51.

7. Ibid.

Chapter 7. The Tide Begins to Turn

1. Jeremy Cohen, *Congress Shall Make No Law* (Ames, Iowa: Iowa State University Press, 1989), p. 118.

2. Ibid.

3. Ibid., p. 111.

4. Robert J. Wagman, *The First Amendment Book* (New York: Pharos Books, 1991), p. 63.

5. Ibid.

6. *Debs* v. *United States*, 249 U.S. 211, 213 (1919).

7. Ibid., p. 214.

8. Robert Cooney and Helen Michalowski, eds., *Power of the People* (Culver City, Calif.: Peace Press, 1977), p. 53.

9. *Debs* v. *United States*, 249 U.S. 211, 212–213 (1919).

10. Raymond Arsenault, *Crucible of Liberty* (New York: The Free Press, 1991), p. 38.

11. David M. Rabban, *The Emergence of Modern First Amendment Doctrine* (Chicago: University of Chicago Law Review, 1983), vol. 50, no. 4, p. 1263.

12. Ibid., p. 1264.

13. *Debs* v. *United States*, pp. 214, 215.

14. *Abrams* v. *United States*, 250 U.S. 616, 617 (1919).

15. Wagman, p. 63.

16. *Abrams* v. *United States*, pp. 619–620.

17. Ibid., p. 621.

18. Ibid., p. 617.

19. Ibid., p. 621.

20. Ibid., p. 626.

21. Ibid.

22. Ibid., pp. 628–629.

23. Ibid., p. 627.

24. Ibid.

25. Ibid., p. 628.

26. Ibid.

27. Ibid., p. 630.

28. Ibid., p. 628.

29. Ibid.

30. *DeJonge* v. *United States*, 299 U.S. 353, 357 (1937).

31. Ibid., p. 361.

32. Ibid., p. 365.

33. Ibid., pp. 364–365.

34. *Dennis* v. *United States*, 341 U.S. 494, 499 (1951).

35. Ibid., pp. 502–503.

36. Ibid., p. 510.

37. Ibid., p. 511.

38. *Brandenburg* v. *Ohio*, 395 U.S. 444, 446 (1969).

39. Ibid., p. 447.

40. Ibid., p. 448.

Chapter 8. Actions That Speak Louder Than Words

1. William Manchester, *The Glory and the Dream* (Boston: Little, Brown and Company, 1973), p. 1055.

2. Ibid., p. 1292.

3. 32 C.F.R. Sec. 1617.1 (1962).

4. *United States* v. *O'Brien*, 391 U.S. 367, 370 (1968).

5. Geoffrey R. Stome et al., *Constitutional Law* (Boston: Little, Brown and Company, 1986) p. 1203.

6. Ibid.

7. Ibid.

8. Ibid., p. 1204.

9. Michael Kent Curtis, ed., *The Constitution and the Flag* (New York: Garland Publishing, Inc., 1993), p. 197.

10. *Texas* v. *Johnson*, 491 U.S. 397, 399 (1989).

11. Ibid., p. 400.

12. Texas Penal Code Ann. Section 42.09 (1989).

13. Peter Irons, ed., *May It Please the Court: The First Amendment* (New York: The New Press, 1997), p. 218.

14. Ibid.

15. *Texas* v. *Johnson*, 491 U.S. 397, 400 (1989).

16. Ibid., p. 414.

17. Ibid., pp. 416–417.

18. Ibid., p. 417.

19. Ibid., p. 420.

20. Ibid.

21. Gerald Gunther, *Constitutional Law*, 12th ed. (Westbury, New York: The Foundation Press, Inc., 1991), p. 1246.

22. Ibid., p. 1247.

Chapter 9. Limits on Free Speech

1. *Ward* v. *Rock Against Racism*, 491 U.S. 781 (1989).

2. *Frisby* v. *Schmaltz*, 487 U.S. 474 (1988).

3. *Tinker* v. *Des Moines*, 393 U.S. 503 (1969).

4. Ibid., p. 504.

5. Ibid., p. 509.

6. Ibid., p. 513.

7. *Chaplinsky* v. *New Hampshire*, 315 U.S. 568, 571–572 (1942).

8. Ibid.

9. Ibid.

10. *Brockett* v. *Spokane Arcades, Inc.*, 472 U.S. 491 (1985).

11. *Pope* v. *Illinois*, 481 U.S. 497 (1987).

12. Robert J. Wagman, *The First Amendment Book* (New York: Pharos Books, 1991), p. 110.

13. *Cohen* v. *California* 403 U.S. 15 (1971).

Chapter 10. The Future of Freedom of Speech

1. Andy Newman, "New M.T.A. Rules on Ads Anger Civil Libertarians," *The New York Times*, October 1, 1997, p. B3.

2. Ibid.

3. Ibid.

4. Ibid.

5. Jan Hoffman, "Testing the Limits of Punishment: Unusually Severe Life Sentence vs. Society's Need For Safety," *The New York Times*, October 27, 1997, p. 31.

6. Ibid.

7. Ibid.

Glossary

appeal—Request to a court with greater authority to review the decision of a lower court. There are two levels of appeal available in state and federal courts. The first is from the trial court to the intermediate court. The second is usually from the intermediate court to the state supreme court. The Supreme Court of the United States is the highest appellate court.

Articles of Confederation—The agreement that bound the American states together directly after the Revolutionary War. The articles resulted in a loose association of the states.

Bill of Rights—The first ten amendments to the United States Constitution. These amendments keep state and federal governments from becoming too powerful. They guarantee that certain rights will be protected, such as the right to freedom of speech.

conscription—Drafting, or enrolling, soldiers into necessary service in the armed forces.

dissent—An opinion written by any Justice who disagrees with the majority in a particular case. Dissenting opinions give a judge's reasons for disagreeing with the majority.

felony—A serious crime, such as murder, for which a violator can be sentenced to more than one year in prison.

fighting words—Words that cause injury simply by being spoken or that tend to bring about an immediate breach of the peace.

First Amendment—The amendment to the Constitution that guarantees freedom of speech, religion, and the press, and the right to assemble peacefully.

Jehovah's Witnesses—A religious group that believes in the second coming of Christ. Members will not serve in the military or take oaths of allegiance.

jurisdiction—The power of a particular court to hear a certain case.

Ku Klux Klan—A group that does not favor equal treatment for Americans who are not white Anglo-Saxon Protestants. The group was organized shortly after the Civil War, and has focused its attacks mainly on African Americans and Jews.

labor union—A group of workers that has been formed to protect and promote the rights of its members.

majority—The written opinion of a court in which the greater part of the deciding judges agree.

per curium—A decision by the entire court. No single Justice claims authorship.

picket—One or more people belonging to a labor union standing outside the place of business to show protest against the company's working conditions or pay. Pickets can also be used to demonstrate political protest.

prosecutor—The person who starts a criminal proceeding against a defendant. The prosecutor also takes charge of the case and acts as the trial lawyer on behalf of the people.

sedition—Stirring up rebellion against the government.

socialism—A theory that all members of a society should share in the production of goods and in the society's wealth.

strike—Members of a labor union refusing to work until management grants better pay or working conditions.

Yiddish—A language that comes from medieval German and is written in the Hebrew alphabet.

Further Reading

Colbert, David, ed. *Eyewitness to America.* New York: Pantheon Books, 1997.

Curtis, Michael Kent, ed. *The Constitution and the Flag.* New York: Garland Publishing, Inc., 1993.

Hentoff, Nat. *Free Speech for Me—But Not for Thee.* New York: HarperCollins Publishers, 1992.

Irons, Peter, ed. *May It Please the Court: The First Amendment.* New York: The New Press, 1997.

Tedford, Thomas L. *Freedom of Speech in the United States.* New York: McGraw Hill, Inc., 1993.

Zinn, Howard. *A People's History of the United States.* New York: HarperPerennial, 1995.

Internet Addresses

The Freedom Forum
<http://www.freedomforum.org/>

Schenck v. *United States*
http://library.advanced.org/11572/cc/cases/schenck.html>

Index